# Gin Soaked Devil: Selected Po
# Thom Young

1)
she was a nomad
going from man to man
breaking hearts
and ruining lives
the past and the future
and
playing the victim
her restless soul
born
free

2)
there are girls
and boys
and love
in
the incessant dream
that
forever
haunts
the broken hearted

3)
gravity always wins
she'll grow up
someday
with
white lace

and the promise
of
love
but the years will
pass her by
with a bitter pill
for the stranger
she thought she
knew
but rest your head
little girl
some nightmares
were always meant
to be.

4)
they wanted more
than the day to day
a sad song
and dirge
for those that danced
on black clouds
until one day
they were gone
and those left
cried for no reason
at
all.

5)
she was a dreamer
and her old friends and life
were past her
now
the tears were there
but
they cried for another girl
they were too late
she tasted eternal love
and had found her home

amongst
the heavens
now.

6)
dogs of love
and hell
and broken lives
where every hurtful
word
is like a razor blade
shining and pure
until
there was nothing left
to cut
but the past.

7)
at night
I hear her
next
to me
and her heart
beats
with mine
despite the distance
and impossibility
of it all
someday
will always
smile.

8)
all the dead fish
can't be wrong
they
know death comes
slowly
and drowns
in what

might have been
and if she gets
away
let her go
with the tide
in and out
and in and out
for
the end often
comes in silence.

9)
among the dead flowers
are
the men of her past
and the heroes
of old
curse her name
from the grave
it wasn't so much her
beauty that killed
but
her fragile smile
over the centuries
mistaken
for love.

10)
from the moment
of
the birth
someone needs to pick up the trash,
wipe the shit up from
the dead that breathe,
break the hearts of lovers, taste the guns
in fragile mouths, dream that everything
is in the right place, listen to the slow death of the clock,
write the poems with no chance, tuck her in bed with
starry eyes,
and make a wish for the deluge to come

and open
the putrid skies
of
regret

11)
it's human nature
to
kill
ourselves
over the dirty carpet
and the ashtray
full of used lives, day old cigarettes, and the unborn
children.
but
none of this shall pass until
she opens her arms
 and accepts us for what
we are
beautiful imperfections

12)
your god
hung on a cross
like
a rubber chicken
for the mass
suicide
and it pains even me
to say I'm a believer
but
there is nothing else
amen.
amen.
amen.

13)
green eyes
in her wake
tides of love and hate

in and out and in and out
until the ocean runs
into
what might have been
because she is the past,
present, future, and
mine.

14)
you
want love
but that's your problem
you
want it too bad
give up
get drunk
live life
things have a way of working out
and isn't that what you need?
to fail at love
is to truly have it

15)
all the unknown colors
and all the unknowns
about love
to see her true beauty
you must look beyond
the surface
and to the heavens
where the angels
sigh.

16)
it's ok to write about
the same thing
over and over
over and over
over and over
and a pack of cigarettes

and a bottle of whiskey
over and over
this is love
and this is her
and this is all
over and over and over and over
like a ship without a rudder..
like a ship
without a..

17)
drunk on her
for 58 weeks
and a pack of unfiltered Chesterfields
sometimes
love doesn't make sense
but at least you felt
it
and the magic remained for awhile
and then it was gone
sometimes you have to hurt
to find forever

18)
the last one
and the American dream
on his arm
with her mind full of cotton
and yoga class
and incessant barking dog
named Precious
and her wanting to be an actress
and her dead family
on holidays
and the ring
and I watch her as she goes by
and he smiles like he's got something
and he does
sometimes hell
comes with a pretty smile.

19)
don't blame
me all
I did was re- open
Daddy's scars
the ones already there
they would have come open eventually
so I'm glad that you pick men
just like him
the hate is often what we love
the most
and now it's over
and the rain fell on Sunday
fell
fell
fell.

20)
I met her on a Wednesday
night
I hit her on the back of the head
drug her on up to my place
propped her in my easy chair
and tied her good
placed a ball gag in her mouth
and read her love poems
watched a re-run of Happy Days
the one where the Fonz
jumped the shark
she was quiet
but I laughed
and cried
and sang to her
oh where oh where can my baby be?

21)
on a beach in California
their heads
washed ashore

some with dull black eyes
and some with a gray clear
film on them
and one was a silent picture
for a dead audience
with a few lights out
on the marquee

22)
death likes the last dance
but
you can cheat on her
by
loving
today.

23)
she said goodbye
in a warm bath
with a pretty pink
razor
her legs needed a shave
but
her
heart bled
the most
over the years
without her lover
and at one time
they said
oh, what a cute couple
but the future
slowly drained a different
way.

24)
I don't need love
and I don't need her
she is lost in a cage
with an open door

a bitter pill
a stupid German girl
this is America
this is me
this is the song I hear
in my mind
at night
but
be quiet
it doesn't play on its
own.

25)
bullet in the head
and dreaming
of a green eyed
girl
in a cave
writing ancient poems
that nobody sees
or wants to
but I want to feel her
from the inside
and the outside
and drink her
like the mystic wines
of the centuries
forever
gone.

26)
she lives in California
as beach fossils
decay
under the sad
Hollywood sign
and she'd leave it all behind
for true love
but it never comes
and the ocean knows

and the sun knows
and she knows
a heart breaks
before
it loves.

27)
don't settle
you may never get another
chance
to say
I love you
to the one you dream about
so make it count
breathe in and breathe out
today
is all you've got
and she needs to hear
it
especially from you.

28)
the sun is coming up
and
the bottles are empty
once again
she isn't coming back
but who would want her to now?
maybe me, maybe last year, maybe never,
and
lighting the morning's first
cigarette
helps you realize
it's not me
she's looking for

29)
she cut her head
off with a dull butcher
knife

and I stared into her eyes
black hued and shiny
in the obsidian
sky
then I tossed it in the
ocean
as the fish swam by
swam
by.

30)
there's a reason
for the cold
it's that her heart
has been broken and used
by others
that thought love
was enough.

31)
if this is the last
chance at love
let
us collapse in the sun
and burn as bright
as perfect
diamonds
shiny and alive
for
the unknown
comes
next

32)
I am the American
failure
kissing the sky with a manicured
lawn with skeletons
buried in the back yard
two point five brats

staring at a dull
screen
please don't wake me
please don't
wake me

33)
open wide
and taste the nightmares
the 9 to 5
the paycheck to paycheck
the
one that got away
as the alarm clock
awakens you to a new kind
of
hell.

34)
I lost my mind
today
but
it doesn't matter
the sun is up
and it looks different
almost purple
and a reddish fire
like her hair
and I lost my mind
today in the deluge
while NYC
cops beat the shit
out of any hope
 left.

35)
she's a gin soaked
devil
with a pretty head
and a .38 special

to blow your brains
out
on the RCA TV
bought
at the second hand store
hawking forgotten dreams
and
distant love.

36)
this coffee
and last pack
of cigarettes
are sometimes
my only friends
but's that ok
with her
because the world
often
becomes a heavy stone
upon
pleasant sinners
 skating on thin
ice.

37)
all the dead leaves
and
 a slow dirge
to the death camp
and she loses a hairpin in the trash
at 2am
I hate you, she said.
but I didn't reply
you never loved me, she said.
but I didn't reply
then the door slammed
and she was gone.
but I'm ok.
got a bottle of wine

and two cats that I take
on a walk
even though they hate me
too.

38)
she stayed
even after he was in love
with somebody else
but
even knowing his affair
she had no will to leave
for her cage was the known
and comfort
and although she said someday
the years and dream went by
and I saw her in a picture with him
with the saddest smile
on earth.

39)
people will spend years
with someone they don't love
and watch tv with them
and wake up with them
and laugh with them
and smile with them
and slowly die
with them
until there's nothing
left with them
but regret and what might have been
and right now someone
is saying "I do."
with a fragile smile
and a broken heart.

40)
there is no way
to tell her

I love you
unless you let her know
you can walk at anytime
and whatever
you do
let her say
it
first.

41)
it's happening
again
it's in your
gut.
it's in your
soul.
it's in your heart.
love
is back
and it's going to be
a hell of a ride.

42)
in and out
of my life
for a second, minute, hour, day, decade,
and century.
there is no sense going on
for
when you died
something grew inside
my heart
it was black and smiled
like the devil
and when I saw your grave
this bird flew out
of me
with wings of the past
and they covered
everything

at least that's how I want
to remember
it.

43)
I'd give up
 city life
to chase you
one more time
and get lost
in your brunette hair
like an ocean sick
with heart break
Lana
if you only knew
what you never had.

44)
so far
but I feel so close
can you feel my heart beating
as you lay upon
my chest?
the sound of distant love
broadcasting
on the transmission
of
 a metal radio
sounds that belong in heaven
and
hell
and that's all except
forever
but that takes
time.

45)
everyone is out there
but
I'm still in bed

and I live my life with
no
regrets
sometimes this is what
it
takes
to truly feel
alive.

46)
if you must
go
don't forget
your dirty pair
of panties
under the bed
from the night
our child was
almost conceived
and
remember
the
few days
you thought you were late?
it all seems
like a dream
now
doesn't
it?

47)
when everything
was going alright
you
never
complained
but
as soon
as the dogs of war
came

and built a wall
between
us
the melody didn't
seem
so sweet
and the days turned
into nightmares
that nobody wanted
but
the neighbor
next door
with cross-hairs
in his eyes.

48)
sandy
beaches
and sock hops
cigarettes
and fast cars
finger
fucks and football
games
those were the days
but
nothing is left
but your addiction
and I inhale and exhale
you
like the 1950s
perfect
with maggots
beneath
the facade.

49)
I can feel
you in my heart
and in my soul

and in my bones
the only
one I ever needed
is
not the one for me.

50)
you can have
me
all you want
tonight
but
in the morning
it's a drive
to the desert
and burnt
cigarettes
with madness
riding shot gun.

51)
she picked up
7 prescriptions and five broken
hearts
on the way back
from
the drug store
and that still wasn't
enough
to get rid of her
I guess the only option
left
is
the diamond ring.

52)
Satan
and a pack
of
rubbers

fuck it all
let's
jump off the bridge
tonight
let me do what I please
baby
it will help me
see
the face
of god
for even this pill
is
bitter to swallow.

53)
free range
nothing
recycled lovers
and
bottles
of dreams
ten for a penny
and a knife
ran across
her pretty
throat
relax, it was always
meant to be.

54)
Texas gentleman
and
a pack
of Lucky Strikes
it
seems my luck
has run out
this time
so say a prayer
for me

mother
things often
end with a finger
on
the trigger.

55)
wave the Canadian
flag
and smile
at the ghost
of
the past
France burns for a reason
assholes
and witches
love a good fire
unless they're
in it.

56)
I wonder how you found
out?
was it the ghost
in the hall?
the bloody knife
by
the weeping mynah
bird?
the spider
smiling in
the corner
of my mind?
I'm not
sure if you
know
this
but I'm in love
with you.

57)
when I dream
of
you
everything
seems
fine
almost a perfect
walk
into
hell
which is often
more
than you can ask for.

58)
all you
have to do is listen
to them read
and you know you have nothing
to worry
about.
or read their words
on the bitter page, on the sandy beaches
for her lover
that never arrived
as the glass animals
dance in the shadows
yes
that's all you have
to do.

59)
I grew tired
of
this world
so I decided
to fight the son of a bitch
but
it was no easy

task
so after this realization
I accepted
it for what it
is
it is what it
is
then we shared
a bottle
of wine.
but I still might
get the last
laugh
you never know?

60)
to all my critics
thanks.
I took your advice
and tossed
it
in an empty
bottle of
Cutty Shark
and you can picture
the old timers
long ago
passing dreams
amongst themselves
that
soon went out
with the tide
into
a choppy restless sea
with all the other
disappointments
waiting
on something
worse
than death.

61)
she kept
dancing
in the empty room
that moments
before
was full of laughter,
 hope,
white lace,
and
baby's breath.
but
now only
her
beauty glided
across
the floor
and the angels smiled
and the bombs
dropped on Pakistan
and in Paris
and in Syria
and in homes all over
America
with the televisions
on
a sitcom
about
two broke
girls.

62)
platinum
blondes
and the holes
in the fish net
stockings at
3am with
handshake

drugs in a part
of the city
that most never knew
or
cared to
except the rats
and dogs lost
in the rain.

63)
first I cut off her legs
and then the arms
there was a beauty
in her
that others
didn't have
then I kissed her
goodbye
and threw her in a green dumpster
and the rain fell enough
to let you know it was there
and the light from the pool
hall
called my name
with one more
chance
and a game of eight ball.

64)
it didn't take me by surprise
when she asked
me to put a cigarette
out on her ass
almost as if she wanted
me to burn
it all
to some place else
but she
didn't know where
and I didn't have the slightest

idea
either.

65)
you can't beat
the horses
or the women
all the time
but if you let them
kick your ass
enough
then you're
already beat
and my cigarette
needs to be lit
and my shoes tied
and I wonder
who they like
in the second race?
I won't pick
that one.

66)
I combed back
my greasy hair
when I saw my angel
appear
she was taking orders
at the late night diner
two fried eggs
over
easy
and black coffee
you couldn't see her wings
but she pushed back
that auburn hair
before it dropped into those
obsidian
eyes
a tragic beauty,

with Amber on her name tag
and a smile that could kill
"What do you want?"
I nodded and ordered my
usual
steak and eggs
the cow bloody as hell
and the eggs
runny
Amber came back
and I said thank you
after she topped off the coffee
then I grabbed her in our
final embrace
and threw her on the linoleum
floor
 I managed to get her skirt up
and then the yellow cotton panties
then I rammed her
good
until
the other patrons
applauded
it was an Oscar worthy
performance
but
the funniest
thing
happened,
she was no longer
beneath
me
but
gone.
my angel flew
away to heaven
with
blood on her apron.
and for some reason
I laughed

for the first time
in
a long while.

67)
if you want to destroy
any
chance you have with her
tell
her
you love her
too soon
and she'll slip
away
on a hot summer
day
in the 1960s
as the ice cream truck's
bell
plays
the end.

68)
the waves crashed
into
us
and nothing
happened
but
the
most amazing thing
was
the
sharks
swam by
with
nothing
but murder
on their
minds.

69)
the sexual
act
can be one of the most
beautiful
things on earth
but
it can also open
the gates
of hell
but
yes
she's worth
it.

70)
your love
takes time
but we're all ready
to punch out
and drink
ourselves
to madness
with another
9 to 5
gone and the Bible
study
come Sunday
and the pretty girls
in dresses
and the pretty
girls
in dresses.

71)
welcome
back 1975
we've missed
you

but
you never really
left
and in mild
lime green station wagons
drinking Flavor-ade
spiked
with the decaying
houses
that some still live
in today.

72)
I need you tonight
but
I think
you better
go
for our time
has past
and though there's still
music
it no longer
plays our favorite
song.

73)
some live in prisons
without bars
like birds
with
no cages.

74)
feeling down
and
out
with a lemonade
suicide
and I don't

want you
but
sometimes love
can be a lost cause
when only one
heart is open to what
might have
been.

75)
I'm going to kill
her
with love
and a dull steak
knife
7.99 at the corner store
and start
a punk band
called The Misfits
although
think that name
is
already taken.

76)
why can't we just admit
it?
the world goes by
with an iron fist
and they
watch the evening news
on TV trays
spoken in the eloquent voices
of
mad men
that can't wait
to say everything
is
fine.

77)
don't force
her
to love
you
if anything use
some
nylon rope
and a smile
that says
it's time
my
dear.

78)
she lived across the court
in apt. 34
and I watched her
in the morning
walking to get the paper
with her dog
and don't ask me
the dog's name
because
it was twenty years ago
and she walked liked
god
and the devil
and her cigarette's ash
almost
fell to the earth
and
the little dog laughed
laughed
laughed.
and
now I feel the tears
for
those days
that

seemed to pass
me
by.

79)
it would
be nice
to finish
second
and I would
if only
she was
be
mine.

80)
there
isn't
much you can
do
or
say
when you're in love
with
the one
you can never
have
but
close your eyes
the dream
is
still
there
and that's all
that matters.

81)
she lives in a doll house
with a perfect Victorian
table

and
a black cat
curled up
by the fire
waiting to gnaw
her to the bone.

82)
the treasure
is
not in the sodden
earth
or in a hidden
cave
where she conducts
the black masses
and the animals
scream for blood
although
whose
I don't know?

83)
I'm not
going to eat
out my heart
anymore
but someday
love
will get you
when you least
expect
it
perhaps
when you're taking
a warm
bath
or staring at the sun
for some unknown
reason

84)
living
for tomorrow
never
did
shit for me
but
a loaded gun
and today
helped
me through
the darkest
of times.

85)
Mommy's little
devil
battered and bruised
with pills, cheap wine,
and the forgotten
men
of her
the past
and now she poses
in a wheelchair
for a sea
of idiots
with nothing to do
but kill
the hours
away

86)
with two dollars
and eighty nine cents
she
bought her past, present, and
future.
then

drove away in a used sedan
with
a pink revolver
and
hell in the rearview

87)
girl
it is meant to be
but
the storms
are coming
so hold on tight
and when I say
"Shut up."
Shut up.

88)
it wasn't easy
to
drag
it
to the tar pit
but
when her body
finally
sank
it reminded me
of the time
we got coffee
in New Jersey
and
we laughed about
being
in love.

89)
if you try
hard enough
you can be whatever

you want
to be.
and the lies
continue
each night
glowing in a box
that's nearly
eighty
years old.

90)
never fall in love
unless
you can
share
hell
together.


Thom Young is a writer from Texas. His work has been in The Commonline Journal, 3am magazine, Word Riot, 48th Street Press, and many other places. A 2008 Million Writers Award nominee for his story Perico. He is one of Amazon's most popular poets hitting #1 in Poetry Anthologies on promotions and his latest A Little Black Dress Called Madness hit #1 Poetry in Germany. His books are popular all over the world including his latest GRINDHOUSE which hit #1 Kindle Free Horror four days in a row.

IG @thomyoung